Newbridge Discovery Links®

PENGUINS

Neil Sims

Newbridge

A Haights Cross Communications Company

Penguins
ISBN: 1-58273-718-5

Program Author: Dr. Brenda Parkes
Content Reviewer: Dyan deNapoli, Penguin Aquarist, New England Aquarium, Boston, MA
Teacher Reviewer: Jennifer Goldenberg, Stevenson Elementary School, Burbank, CA

Written by Neil Sims
Editorial and Design Assistance by Curriculum Concepts

Newbridge Educational Publishing
333 East 38th Street, New York, NY 10016
www.newbridgeonline.com

Cover Photograph: Rockhopper penguin
Table of Contents Photograph: Emperor penguins

Photo Credits
Cover: Frans Lanting/Minden Pictures; Contents page: B & C Alexander/Photo Researchers, Inc.;
pages 4–5: Tui De Roy/Minden Pictures; page 6: Tim Davis/Photo Researchers, Inc.; page 7: (top)
Daniel J. Cox/Natural Exposures, (bottom) Mitsuaki Iwago/Minden Pictures; page 9: Tui De Roy/Bruce
Coleman, Inc.; pages 12–13: Graham Robertson/Auscape; page 13: Kjell Sandved/Photo Researchers, Inc.;
page 14: Frans Lanting/Minden Pictures; page 15: Frans Lanting/Minden Pictures; pages 16–17: Tui De
Roy/Minden Pictures; page 17: Frans Lanting/Minden Pictures; page 18: Andris Apse/APSEA/Bruce
Coleman, Inc.; page 19: Frans Lanting/Minden Pictures; page 20: Frans Lanting/Minden Pictures; page 21:
D. Puleston/Photo Researchers, Inc.; pages 22–23: Hubert Stadler/CORBIS; page 23: Tui De Roy/
Minden Pictures; page 24: (top) George Lepp/CORBIS, (bottom) Tui De Roy/Minden Pictures;
pages 24–25: (background) Tui De Roy/Minden Pictures; page 25: (bottom) Frank Lane Picture Agency/
CORBIS; page 26: Jean-Marc La Roque/Auscape; page 27: Hans Reinhard/Bruce Coleman, Inc.;
pages 28–29: Daniel Zupanc/Auscape; page 29: Tom McHugh/Photo Researchers, Inc.; page 30: Frans
Lanting/Minden Pictures.

Map on pages 10–11 by Susan Johnston Carlson

10 9 8 7 6 5 4 3

Table of Contents

Is That a Bird or a Fish?

You might have seen penguins at the zoo, standing stiffly upright, looking as if they're wearing black-and-white tuxedos. But to see them in the water is to witness an amazing transformation. The funny, flightless penguin turns into a super athlete.

Underwater, the penguin seems more like a fish than a bird. In 1620, Admiral Beaulieu, a European explorer, sailed to Africa and saw penguins for the first time. The birds were darting through the water, and the admiral wondered if they were feathered fish. The penguin's wings, useless in the air, become underwater oars that allow it to "fly" through the sea, fast enough to catch many of the sea creatures it wants for a meal.

King penguins "fly" through the water on flipperlike wings.

These Adélie penguins flap their wings very fast and leap out of the water. Their leap from water onto land can be at least five feet high!

Getting Around on Land

All types of penguins swim with style and skill. But they also spend time on land. What techniques have they developed to get around when they're not in the water?

Penguins use their beaks, claws, and strong legs to help them move about. They can leap out of the water onto the ice, climb onto rocky cliffs, and walk for miles.

When a penguin gets tired of walking or running on Antarctica's slick ice, it will simply flop down on its belly and slide. Pushing itself along with its feet, it can scoot along much faster than by walking. Its claws grab the ice and send the penguin sliding forward with ease.

To save energy, penguins alternate between walking and tobogganing on the ice.

They might look awkward to us, but penguins can actually run faster than people over snow and rocks.

Features of a Penguin

Scientists believe that penguins **evolved** from birds that could walk, fly, and swim. Over millions of years, they lost their ability to fly. Their shape changed, their feathers got shorter and denser, and they became even stronger swimmers. They also developed other adaptations that make them very well suited for the water.

All penguins are rather plump, and when they swim, their fat helps to keep them afloat. But unlike most other birds, penguins have heavy bones that help them dive deep underwater.

Their feathers are designed especially for water and warmth. A penguin's feathers are short and overlapping, forming a windproof and waterproof surface. The tufts of down at the base of each feather trap air, which provides lifesaving warmth. Penguins have more feathers than most other birds on Earth.

To communicate, penguins use different sounds that mean different things. They use one sound to call out to each other at sea, and they use another sound to defend their homes on land.

Its EYES can see very well underwater. It can see the green, blue, and purple colors of the sea.

Its STREAMLINED BODY helps it move through water with ease.

Its BEAK is sharp and is designed to hold onto slippery underwater prey such as squid and fish.

Its LEGS are far back on the body. They work with the tail as a rudder to help them steer.

Its WINGS have evolved to be strong and stiff for underwater movement.

Its CLAWS are sharp and very strong. They are made to grip rock and ice, and dig nests.

Where Penguins Live

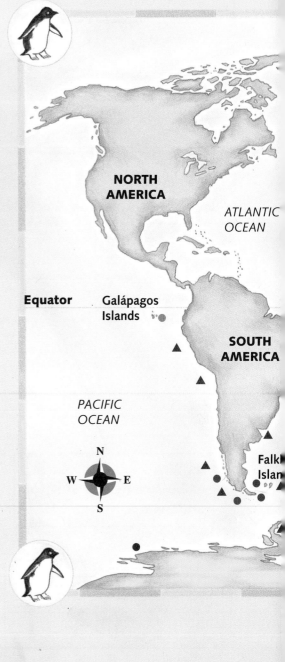

There are 17 different kinds of penguins, and this map shows the different parts of the world in which they live. Many people think that penguins live at both the North and South Poles, but this isn't true. All penguins live south of the **equator**, except for the Galápagos penguins, which live right along the equator.

Get ready to visit four very different places and read about four very different kinds of penguins.

First stop: Antarctica . . .

NORTH
AMERICA

ATLANTIC
OCEAN

Equator   Galápagos
            Islands

SOUTH
AMERICA

PACIFIC
OCEAN

N
W   E
S

Falk
Islan

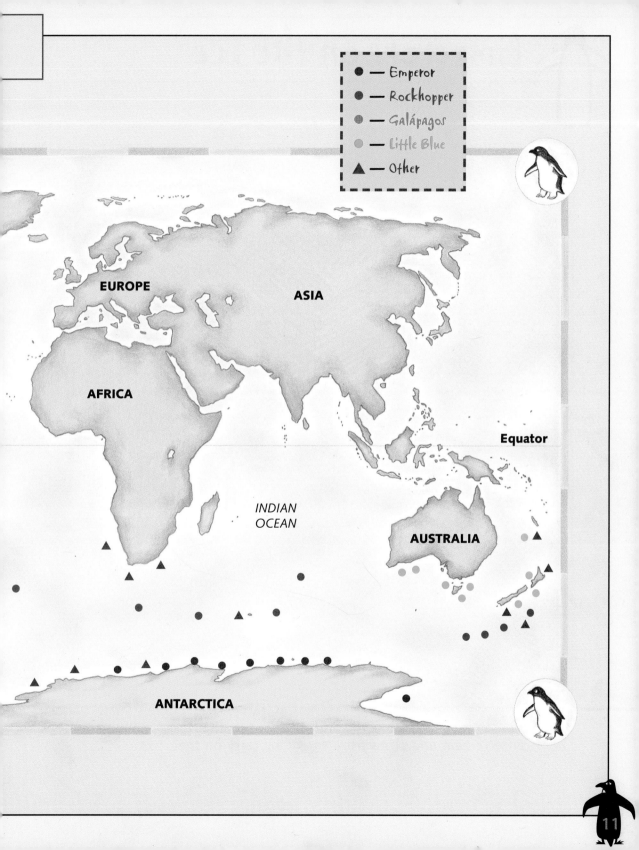

Emperor
Rockhopper
Galápagos
Little Blue
Other

EUROPE

ASIA

AFRICA

Equator

INDIAN
OCEAN

AUSTRALIA

ANTARCTICA

Emperors on the Ice

Thousands of male emperors may huddle together to conserve heat and protect the eggs they carry on their feet.

A winter storm is raging in Antarctica. Icy winds blow snow in tiny tornadoes, at speeds of 50 miles per hour. The ground is solid ice, and the air temperature is 40°F below zero! In the distance, you can see what looks like a carpet of black bumps piercing through the snow. These are the heads of thousands of emperor penguins, huddled together for warmth, calmly waiting out the storm.

Emperors are the largest penguins and are built to survive the cold. They stay on the Antarctic continent for the entire winter. Most others **migrate** to warmer climates during the coldest months.

With a thick layer of fat, and waterproof and windproof feathers, emperors are built to survive the Antarctic winter.

Bringing up Baby

Unlike most other penguins, which lay two eggs, emperors lay only one. After the female lays the egg, it is the male that cares for it all by himself, for 65 days. He tends to it all winter long, keeping it on top of his feet and tucked inside a flap of loose, warm skin on his belly. Until the egg hatches, the father neither eats nor wanders away.

The female is out at sea fattening up. She'll return for her turn to care for the chick when the egg hatches. The male may lose half his weight while incubating the egg. However, once his mate returns to relieve him, he will depart for the sea to feed and fatten up.

Once the chick gets a little bigger, it joins all the other chicks in a group called a **crèche**. By grouping together like this, the chicks stay warmer.

While on the ice, this female emperor tips back on her heels and tail so that her baby doesn't make contact with the ice. Otherwise, the baby would quickly freeze and die.

This adult emperor is looking for its baby in the crèche.

The chicks constantly move from the outer edges inward to take turns being in the warmer center. The grouping also allows both parents to hunt for food. When its parents return from the sea, the chick gets fed by both of them. Parents and their chicks can always find each other because they recognize each others' voices.

This adult emperor and youngsters are on an ice floe. The young penguins are molting and will soon have all their waterproof feathers.

As the chicks get a little older, they will lose their downy feathers, or **molt**, growing new juvenile feathers which are waterproof. The penguins at this stage are called **fledglings**. While molting, they will remain on the ice, never venturing into the water. Like all penguins, they won't be safely

The leopard seal has powerful jaws lined with sharp teeth, and penguins are one of its favorite foods.

insulated or waterproof until they have a complete set of juvenile feathers. By the time their feathers grow in, the penguins will be ready to dive into the water. The next time they molt, they will grow their more colorful adult feathers.

Emperors can survive the cold, but they still have predators. The most dangerous of these is the leopard seal, which can weigh 800 pounds.

Although emperors spend their entire lives in Antarctica, most other kinds of penguins are not found there.

Next stop on your tour: the Falkland Islands . . .

Rockhopper penguins couldn't be more different from emperors. You can easily recognize a rockhopper by the yellow-and-black tufted feathers on its head. Rockhoppers are small, weighing only about 7 pounds compared to the emperor's 85 pounds. They don't live on the ice, but among the rocky cliffs and rough seas of the Falkland Islands, off the coast of Argentina. They also live on the sub-Antarctic islands that circle the globe. And they hop almost everywhere they go.

They can dive very deep, but catch most of their food near the surface of the water. They like to eat tiny sea creatures called **krill**.

One way rockhoppers maintain their bond is by grooming one another.

Like emperors, rockhoppers are wary of leopard seals. Here, a group of rockhoppers watch for danger as one of their braver flock members takes the plunge!

One Tough Bird

Rockhoppers are one of the most aggressive species of penguins, and will not tolerate intrusion from a predator like the *skua*. Though the skua looks like a dark brown seagull, it can be as fierce and powerful as a hawk or an eagle. The skua gives out a blood-curdling scream as it dives toward a rockhopper in its nest. But the rockhopper is one tough bird. It will hold its ground, even jumping up to try to strike the skua on its swoop to the nest.

The rockhopper female lays two eggs, though only one is incubated. Both parents take turns incubating the egg and feeding the chick when it hatches.

Skuas will steal penguin eggs and chicks if they get the chance.

Rockhoppers don't nest on ice as emperors do, but prefer rocky cliffs or mounds of earth like these for their nests.

In the colder areas of their range, rockhoppers are careful to keep their eggs and chicks warm. In the warmer northern parts of their range, they find ways to keep their chicks cool.

Unlike the rockhopper, who adjusts to both hot and cold temperatures, another kind of penguin lives only where it's very hot.

Next stop on your tour: the Galápagos Islands . . .

Galápagos Penguins in the Sun

The desertlike environment of the Galápagos Islands supports a surprising amount of wildlife, both in the sea and on land.

nlike the emperor penguins' world of ice, or the rockhoppers' cool islands, Galápagos penguins have adapted to life on and around islands that are very hot and dry.

With their insulating feathers and fat, how do Galápagos penguins stay cool in the 85°F heat? They spend most of the day in the cool water, coming ashore in the evening and returning to the sea at dawn. Galápagos penguins protect their eggs and chicks from the hot sun by keeping them in deep crevices in the rocks and hardened lava. Unlike human beings, penguins don't have sweat glands. One way they avoid getting overheated is to open their mouths and **pant**, in much the same way as a dog does. Another way these penguins stay cool is by holding their wings out away from their bodies. They also lose heat from the bare skin around their beaks.

Amazing Neighbors

The islands inhabited by the Galápagos penguins are called Las Encantadas by the Ecuadorians who live there. Las Encantadas means "The Enchanted Ones," and these islands really do seem to be enchanted.

Not only do these interesting penguins live there, but they have some amazing animals as neighbors: lizards that swim in the sea, stately birds with sky-blue feet, and tortoises that get as big as boulders.

It is now time to leave this enchanted place and go to the final stop on your tour: Australia and New Zealand . . .

The marine iguana is the only lizard that lives off the ocean, eating algae and seaweed.

Blue-footed boobies are a common bird in the Galápagos.

These colorful Sally Lightfoot crabs would be happy to snatch an egg or a nestling, so the penguins guard their nests carefully.

Galápagos tortoises can weigh 500 pounds and live to be 150 years old!

Little Blues

Tourists from all over the world go to southern Australia just to see the parade of little blues arrive from the sea every evening and march to their burrows.

These little blues will soon take off to hunt for the small fish and squid they love best.

The smallest of the penguins are called little blues. These penguins, more than any other, have colonies close to where people live. This is not because little blues like to be near people. They are actually very shy, and prefer to be left alone. Instead, it's because people have moved into their territory in Australia and New Zealand. It is not uncommon to find a penguin near a house or in a yard.

Like Galápagos penguins, little blues spend all day at sea. They are out at sunrise and hunt for food until evening.

True Blue

All penguins have a small blue spot near the tip of every feather. But on little blue penguins, the spot is quite large, giving them a shiny blue-gray coat.

Little blue penguins stand about 40 centimeters high and weigh 2–3 pounds.

Like other penguins, little blues preen their feathers to keep them clean and waterproof. They do this by rubbing a tiny drop of oil from a special gland above the tail onto each and every feather.

For the most part, little blues and people get along. However, populations of little blues may be declining due to pollution and predators that are not native to the area. These predators include cats, dogs, foxes, and snakes.

But for now, out at sea at dusk, sailors can hear the call of the little blues. And on land, people can watch them arrive every evening as they head for their nests and hungry chicks.

Like many other kinds of penguins, little blues mate for life.

Penguins and People

Each kind of penguin has its own amazing ways to survive. Penguins have adapted to their different environments and developed successful ways of getting around on land and water. Penguins can teach us about surviving in some very cold and very warm places on Earth. Who knows what we can learn from penguins in the future?

Some people visit icy Antarctica just to see penguins up close.

GLOSSARY

crèche: a group of young penguins who huddle together for protection and warmth while their parents are away getting food

equator: the imaginary line that circles Earth halfway between the North and South Poles

evolve: to change gradually over a period of time

fledgling: a young bird that has lost its downy feathers and is growing its juvenile feathers

krill: very tiny sea creatures with hard shells; a favorite food of some penguins and whales

migrate: to journey to another location and back again, following the change of seasons

molt: to naturally lose and regrow feathers, fur, or skin

pant: to take rapid, heavy breaths

Websites

To learn more about penguins, check out:

www.terraquest.com/va/science/penguins/penguins.html

www.seaworld.org/Penguins/home.html

www.livewave.com/viewermain.asp?camera=18

INDEX